RAMBLEWOOD

MANUFACTURING, INC.

Customized Fencing For Business And Home

Second Edition

Job-Order Costing with Just-In-Time (JIT) Inventory

A COMPUTERIZED BUSINESS SIMULATION

Leland E. Mansuetti
Keith Weidkamp

Both of Sierra College

IRWIN

Chicago • Bogotá • Boston • Buenos Aires • Caracas
London • Madrid • Mexico City • Sydney • Toronto

Printed in the United States of America.

ISBN 0–256–17813–5 (5.25'' version)
ISBN 0–256–17807–0 (3.5'' version)

2 3 4 5 6 7 8 9 0 P 2 1 0 9 8 7 6

DEDICATED TO OUR FAMILIES

Janet

Linda, Aaron, Kristin, Zachary

ACKNOWLEDGMENTS

Karen Mahoney

Mitchell Ford and Jennie Novak

The Accounting Students of Sierra College
Rockland, California

PREFACE

The **Ramblewood Manufacturing, Incorporated** computerized practice set has been designed to reinforce the learning of financial accounting and to provide an opportunity to practice decision making and analytical skills needed in a financial and cost accounting environment. The student is given an opportunity to work with a computerized job cost accounting system that reinforces the major concepts of using JIT inventory. Because of the speed and efficiency of the computer system, this reinforcement and practice occurs within a financial accounting environment. The student handles all of the operational transactions of the business for the final month of the quarter including adjustments and financial statements. This allows for a full review of the financial accounting fundamentals including multiple job cost accounting transactions and documents. The computer quickly and efficiently handles all of the time consuming bookkeeping tasks and statement preparation and allows the student time for document and statement evaluation and decision making. While working this business simulation the student will become familiar with a computerized accounting system similar to commercial systems found in the business world.

Sophisticated, yet easy to use, software will allow the student to work very rapidly and efficiently through a variety of job cost and financial accounting transactions. At the end of each data entry session (six or seven days/eighteen to thirty transactions), the student will find a convenient **"Check It Out"** block to compare account balances and trial balance totals. Additional check figures will be presented at some check points for specific job cards. This will include totals for materials, labor, and overhead. If errors are found, the student will simply follow the clear audit trail provided, locate the error/s, and then make the necessary corrections. After the June 10-16 data entry session, and at the completion of the adjusting entries at the end of June (end of the quarter), the student will be asked to print several documents for evaluation. **Mid-project** (June 16) and **Final-project evaluation questions** (June 30) will then be completed using the documents to answer a series of analytical questions. This process will provide a detailed review of the job cost and financial information for the business. Time originally spent preparing job cost documents will now be spent previewing, analyzing, and making decisions and calculations from the information available in the documentation.

The Ramblewood Manufacturing, Inc. computerized accounting system is menu driven. Data entry is accomplished using a general journal screen for journalizing and validation. Pull down screens for the chart of accounts, job card list, customer list, and vendor list are accessible with a single keystroke. Printing of documents for review and analysis is quick and easy. The journal, general and subsidiary ledgers, trial balance, and all job card data can also be brought to the screen for quick review. A **special feature** of the practice set is the **automatic closing process** option which allows the student to close the books quickly and efficiently with a single keystroke. The closing entry procedure, which is so time consuming when completed manually, is similar to many commercial systems. **A reinstatement option** allows the student to reopen the accounts, if necessary, for error correction purposes.

The overall objective of this practice set is to provide students an opportunity to use, learn, and review a tremendous amount of cost accounting and financial accounting information, transactions, and cost and financial documents in a very short period of time. Using this computerized accounting system allows the students to fully realize this objective, maximize their study time, and to move closer to the real world accounting environment.

Leland Mansuetti
Keith Weidkamp

TABLE OF CONTENTS

Preface v

Table of Contents vii

Introduction to Ramblewood Manufacturing, Incorporated 1

Chart of Accounts 2

Customer and Vendor Lists 9

KEY DETAILS TO REMEMBER AS YOU JOURNALIZE TRANSACTIONS . . . 10

Transactions for June 3-9 13
- Boot The Disk And Enter The Data 15
- "Check It Out" Block 26
- Check The Job Cards 27

Error Correction Procedures 28
- Journal Entry Correction 28
- Job Card Correction 29

Transactions for June 10-16 31
- "Check It Out" Block 40
- Print List 41

MID-PROJECT EVALUATION, June 16, 1997 43

Transactions for the Week of June 17-23 51
- "Check It Out" Block 60

Transactions for the Week of June 24-30 61
- "Check It Out" Block 71

Adjusting Entries For the Quarter, June 30, 1997 73
- Print List 76
- Closing Entries 76
- Error Correction After Closing the Books 77

FINAL EVALUATION, June 30, 1997 79

Appendix 89

INTRODUCTION TO

RAMBLEWOOD MANUFACTURING, INC.

Ramblewood Manufacturing, Inc. is a small corporation, locally owned by several investors with the principal stockholders being Ivan Krajewski, Lon Chun, and Delmar Lorzenetti. These three are also the very skilled welding and fabricating craftsmen who work the business full time. The business is located in an industrial park near Rocklin, California. All facilities are leased, and manufacturing equipment is both leased and owned by the corporation. Ramblewood specializes in custom made fencing and gates at prices that are very competitive. The products are made-to-order and are manufactured in a timely and efficient manner. The company is well known throughout the valley area for top quality work at a reasonable price. They are also known to have the equipment, skill, and labor to handle any job large or small.

To complete the on-the-job training requirement for your accounting course you have been placed in a four-week internship program with Ramblewood Manufacturing, Inc. You will be responsible for all of the accounting work from June 3 through June 30 including recording the accounting transactions and time tickets, auditing your work, and correcting all errors. You will also be responsible for the preparation and/or printing of many documents as you work each week as well as the financial statements at the end of the second quarter. Your responsibility will also include the closing of the books at the end of the quarter, and a thorough analysis of the business operations. Since Ramblewood Manufacturing, Inc. uses a computerized accounting system, you will have the opportunity to work with the general ledger, an accounts payable and accounts receivable ledger, job cards, and experience the use of a JIT (Just In Time) inventory system. This opportunity to obtain hands on computer experience and practice your Cost and Financial Accounting skills should be a very rewarding and exciting learning experience.

The first step in operating the computerized system correctly is to review the chart of accounts. A **clear understanding** of how certain accounts are used by Ramblewood Manufacturing, Inc. **is required before you begin the recording process**. A detailed explanation of how several accounts are used in this accounting system follows on the next three pages. Pages 6, 7, and 8 list the full Chart of Accounts and page 9 displays the customer list and vendor list with the account numbers used to identify these individuals and businesses when entering transactions. A summary of the special keys, computer procedures, and business details begins on page 10.

CHART OF ACCOUNTS

To properly enter the accounting transactions for Ramblewood Manufacturing, Inc. you will need to familiarize yourself with the chart of accounts for the business. All revenues earned from the sale of manufactured products are recorded in the **Custom Fencing and Gate Sales** account. Sales are made for cash, on account, and occasionally small sales are made to customers who use **bank credit cards**. When a customer uses a bank credit card to pay for products the sale is entered as a **cash sale.** The credit card expense **is not** recorded at the time of sale. Bank card charges (1%-4%) are recorded monthly when a bank statement is received from the bank. Company credit cards are not currently accepted by Ramblewood Manufacturing, Inc.

Ramblewood Manufacturing, Inc., records all direct and indirect materials purchases at net amounts. All purchases of materials will be on credit. Unless stated otherwise, all invoice information displayed for data entry will be presented and recorded at **NET amounts.** Ramblewood Manufacturing, Inc., expects to take every discount offered by vendors and uses this control system to insure that this occurs for every discount opportunity. If a breakdown occurs in this control system, the amount of the discount lost for failing to pay the vendor within the discount period will be charged to the **Discounts Lost** account.

Ramblewood Manufacturing, Inc., uses a ***Just-In-Time*** (JIT) inventory system. Purchased raw materials, upon arrival at Ramblewood Manufacturing, are placed directly into the production area (factory) for processing, and their cost is charged to an account titled Raw and In-Process Inventory. This eliminates the need to maintain a Raw Materials Inventory account, as in the traditional Job-order cost system where purchased raw materials are charged to a Raw Materials Inventory account.

Direct labor is charged to the Raw and In-Process Inventory account on payroll dates (on the basis of time tickets); and overhead is allocated to the account at a predetermined overhead rate of 80% of direct labor costs, at the end of the accounting period. Job cards are maintained for each job in process.

The Ramblewood Manufacturing JIT system also requires a change from the traditional when dealing with finished goods. Materials are ordered and production begins only when there is a confirmed sales order. Upon completion, the production cost of the job is charged to the Cost of Goods Sold account and credited to the Raw and In-Process Inventory account; thus, eliminating the need for a Finished Goods inventory account. When the product is delivered to a customer (usually within one day of completion), the sale is recorded with a debit to the Cash or Accounts Receivable account and a credit to the Custom Fencing and Gate Sales account.

On some custom orders the customer may be required to pay a cash deposit to initiate the order. Since these custom jobs are normally completed in three weeks or less, the cash deposit is recorded as a **debit to Cash and a credit to Accounts Receivable**. When the job is completed and delivered the Accounts Receivable account is debited for the entire amount of the bill, thus clearing the temporary credit balance of the customer's account. **If any customer has a credit balance at the end of the quarter, this balance is transferred to the Unearned Revenue account through the adjusting entry process.**

Several accounts which require special attention are listed below:

103 **Short-Term Investments** is the current asset control account representing the total of short-term, marketable securities held by Ramblewood.

105 **Accounts Receivable** is the control account for all customer accounts. For special orders the account will be credited for cash deposits made by the customer. Any deposits on jobs not completed at the end of any quarter are transferred to the Unearned Revenue account with an adjusting entry.

113 **Interest Receivable** is normally used only for adjusting entries.

115 **Raw and In-Process Inventory** is debited for the purchase of all direct materials. Under a **JIT (Just In Time) inventory system**, a perpetual inventory of direct and indirect materials will <u>**not**</u> be maintained. ***Materials will be ordered as needed for each job or project.***

124 **Prepaid Rent** is debited for rent payments made for more than one month.

125 **Prepaid Property Tax** accounts for all property taxes paid in advance.

127 **Prepaid Advertising** is used only for adjusting entries. All advertising costs are debited directly to the Advertising Expense account.

129 **Office Supplies** is debited for all purchases of business supplies used in the office.

145 **Leasehold Improvements** to the rented facilities have been made as needed to the manufacturing and warehouse area. A portion of these costs are amortized to the **Manufacturing Overhead** account at the end of each month.

160 **Leasehold** has been debited for a long-term sub-lease. A portion of this leasehold is amortized to **Manufacturing Overhead** at the end of each month.

185 **Manufacturing Overhead** is charged for all indirect materials and indirect labor used in the manufacturing process. **Manufacturing Overhead is also charged for all costs that can be assigned to the manufacturing process. This will include, among others, rent charges applicable to the factory area, shop and factory tools, a prorated share of all utility and telephone expenses, depreciation of shop equipment, property taxes on factory assets, insurance costs on the factory area, leasehold improvements and a prorata share of the leasehold. Manufacturing Overhead is applied to Work In Process at 80% of the Direct Labor Cost.**

221 **Unearned Revenue** is adjusted at the end of the accounting period for any revenues that have been received in advance, credited to the Accounts Receivable account, and at the end of the period have not yet been earned.

231 **Long-Term Lease Liability** accounts for the liability assumed when the capital lease or financing lease for the new shop equipment was signed.

232 **Discount on Lease Financing** is the contra liability account used with the Long-Term Lease Liability account in calculating the carrying value of the capital lease for shop equipment.

311 **Dividends Declared** is debited for all official dividend declarations. At the end of each accounting period the account is closed into Retained Earnings.

401 **Custom Fencing and Gate Sales** is the revenue account of Ramblewood Manufacturing, Inc. All jobs sold for cash, on credit, or to customers using bank credit cards are credited to this account at the time of sale.

501 **Cost Of Goods Sold** is the cost account debited for the cost of each job that has been completed and sold.

601 **Office Supplies Expense** is used only for adjusting entries.

603 **Truck Operating Expense** is charged for all of the operating and repair expenses incurred in maintaining and using the truck for **delivery operations**. The truck is not used in the factory and production side of the business operations.

604 **Advertising Expense** is debited <u>directly</u> for all advertising fees incurred.

607 **Credit Card Expense** accounts for bank credit card fees charged to Ramblewood Manufacturing, Inc., for customer use of their bank cards to pay for manufacturing services. These fees will be between 1 and 4 percent of the total amount of the customer charge. Bank cards are allowed for payment on small custom orders. The total credit card expense will be accounted for monthly upon receipt of a bank statement of the total charges.

621 **Rent Expense** is adjusted for the portion of the Prepaid Rent account applicable to the monthly accounting period. This is done because rent must be charged monthly to the **Manufacturing Overhead** account. A small portion of the Leasehold account is adjusted monthly to the Rent Expense account with the remainder being charged to **Manufacturing Overhead**. All of the leasehold improvements are in the manufacturing area and are amortized to the **Manufacturing Overhead** account.

622 **Insurance Expense** is adjusted at the end of each accounting period.

623 **Bad Debt Expense** is charged for all bad debts that are written off as uncollectible by the business. Ramblewood Manufacturing uses the **Direct Write-off Method** to account for all bad debts.

624 **Property Tax Expense** accounts for the property taxes for the period charged against the assets of the business.

628 **License Expense** is debited for all business and vehicle license fees.

713 **Dividends Earned** is an **Other Revenue** account that is credited for dividends earned on short-term investments.

721 **Gain on Sale of Assets** is an **Other Revenue** account that is credited when the proceeds from the sale of a Plant and Equipment asset are greater than the book value of the asset. This account is **not used** in a like-kind exchange (trade) transaction.

731 **Gain on Short-Term Investments** is credited when the proceeds of an investment sale exceed the original basis of the investment.

814 **Discounts Lost** is an Other Expense account and is charged directly for all discounts lost for failing to pay a materials or supplies invoice within the discount period offered by the vendor.

821 **Loss on Sale/Disposal of Assets** is an **Other Expense** account that is debited when a Plant and Equipment asset is sold and the proceeds of the sale are less than the book value of the asset. This account is also used to account for the loss incurred when the asset with book value is donated or given away. On like-kind exchange (trade) transactions this account is **not used.**

831 **Loss on Short-Term Investments** is debited when the proceeds from the sale of an investment are less than the original basis of the investment.

Entering Transactions And Using The Chart Of Accounts

Special data entry procedures that will make your work very efficient, have been built into the new Ramblewood Manufacturing accounting system. When entering transactions, all of the accounts will be identified by account number. You will see the account title appear instantly on the screen as you enter the account number. With the cursor at the account prompt, the chart of accounts can be displayed on the screen by pressing the **F1** key. The new "quick entry" process is built into the Ramblewood Manufacturing accounting system and will be introduced as you begin to enter the first few transactions.

Customer and Vendor Lists

Detailed information on customer and vendor account activity and balances will be maintained automatically in the Accounts Receivable and Accounts Payable ledgers. Information will be recorded in the system by identifying each customer or vendor/creditor by number. When the customer or vendor prompt appears, the appropriate customer or vendor list will automatically be displayed in the upper left corner of the screen. When you enter the last digit of the customer or vendor number and press the **Enter** key, the list will automatically clear from the screen.

Entering Direct Labor and Manufacturing Overhead

As the work on each custom order progresses, time tickets will report all of the cutting and finishing or welding time charged to that job. This labor information will be entered on the appropriate job card as it is received in the accounting office. The job card menu can be called to the screen by pressing the **F4** key. Specific details for this data entry procedure are explained later in the first week of entries.

CHART OF ACCOUNTS
RAMBLEWOOD MANUFACTURING, INCORPORATED

ASSETS

101	Cash
103	Short-Term Investments
105	Accounts Receivable
109	Notes Receivable
113	Interest Receivable
115	Raw and In-Process Inventory
123	Prepaid Insurance
124	Prepaid Rent
125	Prepaid Property Tax
127	Prepaid Advertising
129	Office Supplies
131	Office Equipment
132	Accumulated Depreciation, Office Equipment
135	Shop Equipment
136	Accumulated Depreciation, Shop Equipment
139	Trucks
140	Accumulated Depreciation, Trucks
145	Leasehold Improvements
160	Leasehold
185	Manufacturing Overhead

LIABILITIES

201	Accounts Payable
203	Notes Payable
204	Discounts on Notes Payable
207	Dividends Payable
209	Salaries & Wages Payable
211	Estimated Property Taxes Payable
213	Income Taxes Payable
215	Interest Payable
221	Unearned Revenues
231	Long-Term Lease Liability
232	Discount on Lease Financing

CHART OF ACCOUNTS
RAMBLEWOOD MANUFACTURING, INCORPORATED

STOCKHOLDERS' EQUITY

301 **Common Stock**
305 **Retained Earnings**
311 **Dividends Declared**

REVENUE

401 **Custom Fencing and Gate Sales**

COST OF GOODS SOLD

501 **Cost Of Goods Sold**

OPERATING EXPENSES

601 **Office Supplies Expense**
602 **Office Salaries & Wages Expense**
603 **Truck Operating Expense**
604 **Advertising Expense**
607 **Credit Card Expense**
611 **Depreciation Expense, Office Equipment**
615 **Depreciation Expense, Trucks**
621 **Rent Expense**
622 **Insurance Expense**
623 **Bad Debt Expense**
624 **Property Tax Expense**
625 **Electric and Gas Expense**
626 **Telephone Expense**
627 **Bank Service Charges**
628 **License Expense**
629 **Professional Services Expense**
631 **Miscellaneous Expense**

CHART OF ACCOUNTS
RAMBLEWOOD MANUFACTURING, INCORPORATED

OTHER REVENUE

711 Interest Earned
713 Dividends Earned
721 Gain on Sale of Assets
731 Gain on Short-Term Investments
741 Miscellaneous Revenue

OTHER EXPENSE

811 Income Tax Expense
813 Interest Expense
814 Discounts Lost
821 Loss on Sale/Disposal of Assets
831 Loss on Short-Term Investments

INCOME SUMMARY

901 Income Summary

Ramblewood Manufacturing, Incorporated
Customer List

Customer Number	Customer
10400	Adams Construction Co.
10650	Berline, Incorporated
10930	Fontaine Storage
11000	Lakeside Pools, Inc.
11150	Ralph E. Maxwell
11460	Sierra College
11680	Sutter County
11910	Wasaki Pool and Spa

Ramblewood Manufacturing, Incorporated
Vendor List

Vendor Number	Vendor
20500	Ambrosini Steel, Inc.
21880	Delta Supply
22500	Golden Welding Supply
23400	Granite Business Supply
24800	Klondyke Air & Gas
25850	Loomis Legal Group
26575	River City Steel, Inc.
28500	Yamasaki Steel, Inc.

KEY DETAILS TO REMEMBER AS YOU JOURNALIZE TRANSACTIONS

To properly and efficiently operate the computerized accounting system used by Ramblewood Manufacturing Inc., you must be familiar with several important computer procedures as well as business and account information details. These procedures and details are summarized in the list below and are introduced and explained in detail in the data entry procedures of the first week of your internship (June 3-9).

The **F1** key may be used at **any account prompt** to display the **Chart of Accounts**. The chart of accounts may be used for faster data entry as well as for a quick reference to the number of each account in the chart of accounts.

The **F4** key will be used to access the Job Cards. Direct labor charges for each job will be entered as the job time tickets are received by the office. As this information is recorded the computer will automatically calculate and enter the manufacturing overhead to the job at 80% of the direct labor costs.

The **F10** key will be used as a part of the "quick journal entry" process. After the debit/s have been entered, this key will automatically enter the amount of the credit entry (last credit entry if more than one credit).

A customer list with customer account numbers will automatically appear on the screen when the Accounts Receivable account is a part of the journal entry.

A vendor list with the vendor (creditor) account numbers will automatically appear on the screen when the Accounts Payable account is a part of the journal entry.

Time Tickets are used to report the total hours and type of work applied to each job. **Welding work** is billed at a rate of **$55.00 per hour** while the **cutting of materials** and **finishing work** is billed at **$44.00 per hour.**

The **Esc** key may be used to exit quickly from all sub menus to the main menu. It may also be used in the **recording procedure to backup and erase an amount or an account.**

Credit Card Fees of **1-4%** will be assessed by banks for customer credit card charges. All bank card sales are considered the same as a cash sale. The credit card fees will be accounted for as a summary entry upon receipt of the monthly bank statement.

When entering transactions, always use proper accounting procedure and enter the debit entries **first**. When **debits** equal **credits** you will have a complete transaction to verify.

When several entries are to be entered on the same day, after the first journal entry has been entered and verified, press the **D** key at the date prompt to automatically enter the date for each subsequent transaction.

Error correction procedures for the Ramblewood Manufacturing system require that the incorrect entry **be backed out (reversed)** and **then reentered correctly**. This correction procedure will be introduced in the first few transactions of the project. When an invoice number prompt, item prompt, or overhead prompt appears when entering a back out entry, enter **ERROR**. If an **error correction entry for cash** requires a credit to cash (and a check is not being issued), enter **ERROR** at the check number prompt. Additional detailed error correction instructions will be presented at the first check point (the end of the first week of transactions).

AT THE END OF EVERY JOURNALIZING SESSION, RETURN TO THE MAIN MENU. This procedure will post all of the transactions to the appropriate ledgers and transfer all data entered during the session from the computer memory to your disk.

You may terminate a journalizing session **at any time.** When you return to the journal entry process at a later time, the last entry recorded will be displayed on the screen.

At the end of each week, audit your work and make all of the necessary corrections required to match the "Check It Out" box. If printed documents are required, you must print the items **before continuing to the next week of transactions**. The system does not store end-of-week balances that can be printed later.

A June 2, 1997 Trial Balance, Schedule of Accounts Receivable, and **Schedule of Accounts Payable** are shown in the Appendix.

RAMBLEWOOD MANUFACTURING, INCORPORATED

TRANSACTIONS FOR JUNE 3 - 9

BOOT THE DISK AND ENTER THE DATA

When you have a good understanding of the accounts used by **Ramblewood Manufacturing, Incorporated,** you are ready to begin the journalizing process. The transactions for your first work week of June (3rd through 9th) follow, and you are encouraged to prepare your account entry information before sitting down at the computer. This procedure will speed up your data entry time. An example of written analysis before data entry is shown on page 16 with the first June 3 transaction.

You may prefer to analyze each entry and record the transaction on the computer at the same time. You will be able to call the chart of accounts, customer list, and vendor list to the screen during the data entry process. This makes the recording of transactions and related information a very quick, easy, and efficient procedure.

IF YOUR COMPUTER HAS A HARD DRIVE AND AUTOMATICALLY DISPLAYS THE C:\> PROMPT: boot the computer and when the **C prompt** (C:\>) appears, place your disk in the appropriate drive **(3-1/2" or 5-1/4")** and make note of the disk drive designation **(Drive A or Drive B).**

IF YOU ARE USING DRIVE A: At the C:\> prompt type A: and press the Enter key. At the **A:\> prompt** type ***RAMBLE*** and press the **Enter** key.

IF YOU ARE USING DRIVE B: At the C:\> prompt type B: and press the Enter key. At the **B:\> prompt** type ***RAMBLE*** and press the **Enter** key.

IF YOUR COMPUTER AUTOMATICALLY EXECUTES WINDOWS: place your disk in the appropriate drive (3-1/2" or 5-1/4") and make note of the disk drive designation **(Drive A or Drive B).**

Click on the MS DOS icon.

IF YOU ARE USING DRIVE A: At the C:\> prompt type A: and press the Enter key. At the **A:\> prompt** type ***RAMBLE*** and press the **Enter** key.

IF YOU ARE USING DRIVE B: At the C:\> prompt type B: and press the Enter key. At the **B:\> prompt** type ***RAMBLE*** and press the **Enter** key.

In a few moments you will see the opening screen for the **Ramblewood Manufacturing, Inc.,** practice set. **Follow the directions presented on the screen.** Enter your name, today's date **(the date you are working the set),** and make any corrections necessary. From the main menu select the **General Journal** option and then the **Journalize Daily Entries** option. When the general journal appears on the screen you are ready to enter the first transaction. Carefully follow instructions 1-6 as you begin the data entry procedure.

TRANSACTIONS FOR THE WEEK OF JUNE 3-9, 1997

Student Analysis

June 3
Issued check number **10551** for $455.00 to the law firm of Ramirez, Alloette, and Cohanna for professional services received. The invoice number for this service billing received today is C4577.

629 455.00
101 455.00

This transaction has not been entered on the disk!

^^

1. ***At the date prompt, for June 3, enter 06 for the month and 03 for the day. When entering any part of the transaction, you may back up and reenter the information by using the backspace key. If you have already entered the data and are on the next item, use the Esc key to back up and enter the correction.***

2. ***At the account prompt, enter 629 to record the debit to Professional Services Expense and enter $455.00 as the amount. Do not use dollar signs or commas. Since the only other account for this transaction is a credit, at the prompt enter C for credit.***

3. ***At the account prompt enter 101 to record the credit to Cash and enter $455.00 as the amount. When debits equal credits, the entry is complete and the check number prompt will appear.***

4. ***At the check number prompt enter number 10551.***

5. ***At the invoice prompt enter C4577 as the billing invoice number.***

6. ***Check the entry carefully. If the entry is correct, enter Y for Yes and proceed to the next transaction. If you wish to make any corrections answer N for No. You may return to three different areas of the general journal to make corrections. Enter D to return to the date, J to return to the journal entry, or N to return to the customer, vendor or document numbers.***

TRANSACTIONS FOR THE WEEK OF JUNE 3-9, 1997

Student Analysis

Continue entering the transactions for the first week. If you discover that a transaction entered into the system at an earlier time needs correction, **simply reverse or back out the error transaction and then enter the data correctly.** More detailed instructions on error correction procedures are given below. A complete summary of the error correction process is presented on page **28**.

^^^

June 3

Discovered that an entry for $49.75 for advertising printing charges had been recorded in error to the Miscellaneous Expense account rather than the Advertising Expense account. The date on the original cash transaction entry is ***June 2*** and the invoice number is **88997**.

1. ***The entry correction procedure for the Ramblewood Manufacturing accounting system requires that each error entry be backed out and then reentered correctly. Using the June 2 date, debit the Cash (101) account and credit the Miscellaneous Expense (631) account for the $49.75. At the item prompt enter ERROR.***

2. ***Since the date of the second transaction is also June 2, press D at the date prompt and the June 2 date will automatically be entered for you. This saves data entry time when several transactions are recorded on the same date.***

3. ***Enter the transaction correctly with a debit to Advertising Expense (604) and a credit to Cash (101). When the check number prompt appears, enter ERROR to indicate that this is an error correction entry and a new check is not being issued. Enter the invoice number (88997) as requested. Additional error correction instructions are found on page 28.***

Note: This error correction procedure leaves a clear audit trail of all corrections and is to be followed throughout this business simulation.

If you wish to display the chart of accounts, press the F1 key at the account prompt. Use the Page Up and Page Down Keys to move through the pages of the chart of accounts. Press the (Esc)ape key to return to the account prompt.

TRANSACTIONS FOR THE WEEK OF JUNE 3-9, 1997

Student Analysis

NOTE: The following time-saving option may be used when journalizing transactions.

AUTOMATIC SUMMATION OF DEBIT ENTRY DOLLAR AMOUNTS

June 4
Purchased on account from Granite Business Supply, office equipment listed at $485.50 and office supplies listed at $35.75. Sales taxes are included in the listed prices of these assets. The invoice number for this transaction is **GB447** and Granite Bay Business Supply offers net 10 credit terms.

After you have entered all the debit entries (one or more), and have entered the account number of the last account to be credited, press the F10 key at the dollar amount prompt and the correct amount will be automatically entered (debits will equal credits).

1. ***At the date prompt, enter 06 for the month and 04 for the day.***
2. ***Debit account 131, Office Equipment, for $485.50.***
3. ***Debit account 129, Office Supplies, for $35.75.***
4. ***Credit account 201, Accounts Payable. When the program requests the amount of the credit, PRESS THE F10 KEY. The sum of the two debits will be automatically entered as the dollar amount for the credit.***

   This feature may be used for both simple entries (one debit account and one credit account), and for compound journal entries at the last account credited.

5. ***At the vendor prompt enter vendor number 23400 for Granite Business Supply. The vendor list will automatically appear in the upper left corner of the screen.***
6. ***At the invoice prompt enter invoice number GB447.***

TRANSACTIONS FOR THE WEEK OF JUNE 3-9, 1997

Student Analysis

NOTE: The following time-saving option may be used when journalizing transactions.

ACCOUNT SELECTION FROM THE CHART OF ACCOUNTS

June 4
Purchased **two** new welding units (Shop Equipment) from Golden Welding Supply. The **list price** of the mobile units is $4,300 **each**, but the units have been discounted 15% for the multiple purchase. The invoice number is **G3344**, credit terms are net 30, and the equipment is shipped FOB destination.

1. ***Enter D for the date and at the account number prompt, press the F1 key. The Chart of Accounts will appear on the screen.***

2. ***Use the PgUp or PgDn keys to move to the page of the chart that contains the number and title of the account to be debited or credited. Move the cursor to the number of the account to be debited (135) and press the Enter key. The account title will automatically be placed on the journal page; the amount prompt will be ready for the dollar entry. Should you access the chart and decide not to use the automatic selection and placement feature, press the (Esc)ape key to return to the account prompt.***

3. ***Select credit for the next entry.***

4. ***Press the F1 key again. Move the cursor to the number of the account to be credited and press the Enter key.***

5. ***Press the F10 key to enter the dollar amount.***

6. ***Enter the vendor number (the vendor list will automatically appear) and invoice number as requested.***

^^

June 4
Received a bill from the Rocklin Bee for a large pictorial ad placed in the Bee this past weekend. Issued check **10552** for $225 as payment in full (invoice number **R9999**).

You may use the D (date), F1 (chart of accounts), and F10 (automatic credit amount) keys for more efficient data entry.

TRANSACTIONS FOR THE WEEK OF JUNE 3-9, 1997

Student Analysis

June 5
Received a check for $36,750.45 from Sutter County as payment in full on their account. The sales invoice number on the sale was **R2020**.

^^

June 5
Purchased direct materials from River City Steel, Inc., to begin **JOB21** for contractor Ralph E. Maxwell. Mr. Maxwell special ordered 60 sections of the Ramblewood custom fencing. The purchase invoice (**M4332**) totals net materials at $23,158.00 and credit terms of net 30. The materials were delivered this afternoon to the Ramblewood factory. Direct materials should be charged to the Raw and In-Process Inventory account.

Stock Number	Quant.	Item Description	Unit Cost	Total
Z0001	550	Ball Ornament	.48	$264.00
Z0110	800	Arrow Ornament	.98	784.00
D0100	1,150	1 In. T W Tube .065	9.00	10,350.00
XX105	20	Electronic Gate Set	588.00	11,760.00
				$23,158.00

^^

June 5
Purchased indirect materials on account from Klondyke Air & Gas and charged the items to the Manufacturing Overhead account. Information from invoice **K1244** lists a total net cost of $353.50. At the **Overhead** prompt enter **INMAT** for indirect materials. Klondyke extends terms of 2/15, n/30.

Stock Number	Quant.	Item Description	Unit Cost	Total
IM060	2	Argon CO2	67.75	$135.50
IM025	1	.035 GS Wire Spool	32.00	32.00
IM032	3	.045 Flux Core Wire	62.00	186.00
				$353.50

TRANSACTIONS FOR THE WEEK OF JUNE 3-9, 1997

Student Analysis

June 5
A custom made gate and side fencing was delivered to customer Ramirez Kevin, COD (sales invoice number **R2045**). A cashiers check for $8,150 was received at the job site. **JOB19** was completed on June 1, and an entry debiting Cost of Goods Sold and crediting Raw and In-Process Inventory has been recorded.

^^

June 6
Received a cash dividend of $.48 (48 cents) per share on the 12,000 shares of Thunder Mountain Snowmobile, Corporation common stock held as a short-term investment. At the item prompt enter **CASHD** for cash dividend.

^^

June 6
The $1,250.65 accounts receivable balance of Fontaine Storage has proven to be uncollectible and is written off. Ramblewood Manufacturing uses the **direct write-off method** for all bad debt write-offs. At the invoice prompt enter **WROFF**.

^^^

June 7
Donated, to the Oakmont High School Shop Class, used welding equipment that has been replaced recently. The shop equipment originally cost $795, has no current market value, and was fully depreciated ($0.00 book value) at the end of last quarter which ended on March 31. At the item prompt enter **DONAT** for donation.

TRANSACTIONS FOR THE WEEK OF JUNE 3-9, 1997

Student Analysis

June 7
A final time ticket (**TT455**) for **JOB20** totals **6.0** hours of finishing time at **$44.00** per hour. **Direct Labor charges are entered directly on each job card.**

1. *At the date prompt press the F4 key.*

2. *Enter the date.*

3. *From the job menu select JOB20.*

4. *Select option A to enter additional Direct Labor costs for JOB20. (Note the menu selections: Option C may be used to correct Direct Labor data in error. Use Option Q if you wish to QUIT the job card and return to the journalizing menu.*

5. *Enter time ticket number 455 and press the Enter Key.*

6. *Enter the 6 hours of labor in a five-digit (00.00) format. Six hours is entered as 06.00. As an example: Six hours and thirty minutes would be entered as 06.50.*

7. *Select (B) for the $44.00 per hour rate for finishing work.*

8. *When the information is correct, enter Y for YES. The Direct Labor will be posted to the job card. When the Direct Labor is verified and posted, the Manufacturing Overhead is automatically entered on the job card at an applied rate of 80% for Direct Labor costs. Note the new totals for Labor and Overhead.*

9. *JOB20 is now complete. Since this is the final entry for JOB20, write the total cost of the completed job here! $____________ This total will be used for the next journal entry.*

10. *Press any key to continue, then select (Q) to Quit JOB20 and return to the job card menu.*

11. *Select (Q) Quit to exit the job card menu and return to the General Journal.*

Specific error correction procedures for the job cards can be found on page 29.

TRANSACTIONS FOR THE WEEK OF JUNE 3-9, 1997

Student Analysis

June 7
Record the transfer of the finished product out of Raw and In-Process Inventory (factory) for shipment to the customer by entering a debit to Cost of Goods Sold and a credit to Raw and In-Process Inventory for the total cost of completing **JOB20** (*See instruction 9 on page* 22). To return to the **JOB20** job card and verify the total cost of the job, press the **F4** key at the date prompt.

^^

June 7
Delivered **JOB20** to the work site for Wasaki Pool and Spa. Sales invoice **R2046** charges $10,250.00 to the account of this customer. The goods are delivered FOB destination.

^^

June 7
Purchased from Delta Supply additional direct materials for **JOB21** (invoice number **D4689**). All prices are shown below at **net amounts** and credit terms offered are 2/10, n/30.

Stock Number	Quant.	Item Description	Unit Cost	Total
XX001	2	Custom Gate Set	424.50	$849.00
Z2011	50	Post Ornament	2.05	102.50
				$951.50

^^

June 8
Issued check number **10553** and paid a cash dividend of **$.15 (fifteen cents) per share** to all June 1 stockholders of record. The dividend was declared on May 15, and is payable today, June 8. The company currently has 100,000 shares of common stock outstanding. At the invoice prompt enter **CASHD** for cash dividends.

TRANSACTIONS FOR THE WEEK OF JUNE 3-9, 1997

Student Analysis

June 8
Purchased additional indirect materials from Klondyke Air & Gas (invoice number **K1299**). Credit terms offered by Klondyke are 2/15, n/30, and prices listed are net amounts. At the overhead prompt enter **INMAT** for indirect materials.

Stock Number	Quant.	Item Description	Unit Cost	Total
IM041	2	280 Oxygen	24.50	$49.00
IM053	2	MSA Acetylene	23.52	47.04
				$96.04

^^

June 9
Purchased direct materials on account (invoice number **Y1332)** from Yamasaki Steel. Yamasaki extends terms of 2/10, n/30, and materials are delivered FOB destination. All items purchased are listed below at **net amounts** and are purchased for **JOB21.**

Stock Number	Quant.	Item Description	Unit Cost	Total
D0100	60	1" T Wall Tube .065	9.00	$540.00
B9625	252	5/8" T Wall Tube .065	5.50	1,386.00
E0150	30	1 1/2" T W Tube .065	14.00	420.00
				$2,346.00

TRANSACTIONS FOR THE WEEK OF JUNE 3-9, 1997

Student Analysis

June 9

Final time tickets for **JOB21** total **32.0** hours of welding time @ **$55.00** per hour (time ticket **TT456**), and **14** hours and **15** minutes of finishing time @ **$44.00** per hour (time ticket **TT457**). **Direct Labor charges are entered directly on each job card.**

1. ***At the date prompt press the F4 key, then enter the date.***

2. ***From the job menu select JOB21.***

3. ***Select option A to enter Direct Labor costs for JOB21. (Note the menu selections: Option C may be used to correct Direct Labor information. Use Option Q if you wish to QUIT the job card and return to the journalizing menu.***

4. ***Enter time ticket number 456 and press the Enter Key.***

5. ***Enter the 32.0 hours of labor in a five-digit (32.00) format.***

6. ***Select (A) for the $55.00 per hour rate for welding work.***

7. ***When the information is correct, enter Y for YES. The Direct Labor will be posted to the job card. When the Direct Labor is verified and posted, the Manufacturing Overhead is automatically entered on the job card at an applied rate of 80% of Direct Labor costs. Note the new updated totals for Labor and Overhead, then press any key to continue.***

8. ***Press A again to add the finish work hours reported on time ticket 457.***

9. ***Enter 14 hours and 15 minutes in a five-digit (14.25) format.***

10. ***Select (B) for the $44.00 per hour rate for finishing work.***

11. ***When the labor information is complete and correct, enter Y for YES. Labor and Overhead costs for this job will show new updated totals.***

12. ***JOB21 is now complete. Since this is the final entry for JOB21, write the total cost of the completed job here! $____________ This total will be used for the next journal entry.***

14. ***Press any key to continue, then press (Q) to QUIT, and return to the job card menu.***

15. ***Again press (Q) to QUIT, exit the job card menu and return to the General Journal.***

TRANSACTIONS FOR THE WEEK OF JUNE 3-9, 1997

Student Analysis

June 9
Record the transfer of the completed fencing for **JOB21** out of Raw and In-Process Inventory. The fencing will be delivered to the R. E. Maxwell job site (sold) at a later date.

^^

Now that you have completed entering the transactions for the first week, June 3-9, **it is time to check the accuracy of your work.** At the date prompt press the **Esc** key and return to the journalizing menu. **To transfer the data from the computer memory to your disk always exit the journalizing process and return to the journalizing menu. Please note that failure to exit the journalizing process before turning off the computer will result in the loss of the data recorded this journalizing session.**

In the "**Check It Out**" block below are the correct balances of key accounts that you have been working with this period. From the main menu select the **General Ledger** option. Then select the **Trial Balance** option and display the document on the screen. Check your figures against the totals shown in the "**Check It Out**" block.

"CHECK IT OUT"

101 Cash	$51,681.20
105 Accounts Receivable	45,700.00
115 Raw and In-Process Inventory	(4,771.80)
135 Shop Equipment	126,915.00
136 Accumulated Depreciation, Shop Equipment	25,705.00
185 Manufacturing Overhead	549.54
201 Accounts Payable	92,606.29
207 Dividends Payable	0.00
501 Cost of Goods Sold	191,691.30
623 Bad Debt Expense	7,500.65
713 Dividends Earned	5,857.00
TRIAL BALANCE	$727,869.90

CHECK THE JOB CARDS

1. Return to the main menu and select the **Subsidiary Ledger** option.

2. From the sub menu select (J), the **Job Cost Ledger** option and select (J) for **Single Job Card**.

3. Select **JOB20** and display the job card on the screen. **JOB20** was sold on June 7. The totals on the **JOB20** card should show:

   A. **$5,355.00** for **direct materials**
   B. **$1,164.00** for **direct labor**
   C. **$ 931.20** for **manufacturing overhead**
   D. **The completed cost of JOB20 is $7,450.20**

   Press any key to continue and return to the job card menu.

4. Select **JOB21** and display the job card on the screen. **JOB21** has been completed and will be delivered on June 10. The job card should total:

   A. **$26,455.50** for **direct materials**
   B. **$ 2,387.00** for **direct labor**
   C. **$ 1,909.60** for **manufacturing overhead.**
   D. **The completed cost of JOB21 is $30,752.10**

   Exit the job cards and return to the main menu. If corrections are needed on a job card, refer to the job card correction procedures outlined on page 29.

IF ALL OF YOUR TOTALS MATCH THE CHECK FIGURES and JOB CARDS, you are ready to enter the transactions for the second week of June or **return** to the main menu and **exit** the system. If any of your balances do not match the check it out block or the **JOB20** or **JOB21** job cards, you have one or more errors that must be corrected before you continue. To correct an account balance, you will need a copy of the general journal to locate and correct the journal entry error/s. To print the general journal select the **General Journal** option from the main menu. From the general journal menu select the **Display/Print the General Journal** option. Select the **"Week One"** option and print all of the journal entries recorded for the first week. If a printer is not available, you may view selected entries on the screen.

If you have several errors, you may also need to print a copy of the trial balance. From the main menu select the **General Ledger** option. From the general ledger sub menu select the **Trial Balance** option and print the trial balance. Then return to the main menu.

If your job card totals do not match the check figures given, carefully check the journal entries involved for the job cards as well as the entries made to record the labor hours directly on the job cards. You may print or view information on each job card through the **Subsidiary Ledger** option on the main menu.

For **accuracy, efficiency,** and **a clear audit trail,** use **ONLY** the correction system designed for the Ramblewood Manufacturing accounting system. ***Any account that is not correct is a MAJOR CLUE for you to check out.*** **Your account balances must match the check figures.**

PLEASE NOTE: Although no printed documents are required for June 9, if you wish ANY June 9 printouts they must be printed BEFORE ENTRIES FOR THE WEEK OF JUNE 10-16 ARE RECORDED. New entries for this period will change the account balances permanently. The Trial Balance and other statements for June 9 are not stored and CANNOT be recalled at a later time.

ERROR CORRECTION PROCEDURES

For the Ramblewood Manufacturing Accounting System

JOURNAL ENTRY CORRECTION

Carefully examine all entries recorded for each period and when an error is found use the following correction procedure:

1. ***Back the transaction out using the date used in the error entry.***

2. ***Enter the correct transaction using the correct date of the original entry.***

If, for example, you discover a June 3 transaction for advertising had been entered in error as a debit to Miscellaneous Expense, simply back out **(reverse)** the error as follows:

June 3	***Cash***	***350.00***	
	Miscellaneous Expense		***350.00***

Using the same June 3 date, record the correct entry.

June 3	***Advertising Expense***	***350.00***	
	Cash		***350.00***

Enter **ERROR** at the check number prompt since this is a **correction** to cash and **does not** involve the issuance of another check.

The error entry, the backout entry, and the correction entry will appear in the accounting records leaving a clear, easy-to-follow audit trail.

When the account balances match those in the **"Check It Out"** block, you are ready to enter the transactions for the next period. If you are finished entering transactions for this session, return to the main menu and exit the system.

JOB CARD CORRECTION

IF YOU RECORDED A TIME TICKET:

A. With an incorrect amount or rate

B. To the wrong job card

1. Return to Journalizing Daily Transactions and at the date prompt press the **F4** key.

2. Enter the date and from the job card menu select the number of the job card that you wish to correct.

3. When the job card is displayed, press **C** (to correct). **Enter the incorrect data EXACTLY AS IT WAS ORIGINALLY RECORDED**, verify and answer **Y** for Yes. This procedure will "back out" the incorrect data.

4. Press **A** and **enter the correct data** on this card, or **Q** to quit if you must select a different job card to make the correct entry.

5. If data needs to be entered on a different job card press the **F4** key, select the correct job card, and continue the entry process using the correct information.

RAMBLEWOOD MANUFACTURING, INCORPORATED

TRANSACTIONS FOR JUNE 10 - 16

TRANSACTIONS FOR THE WEEK OF JUNE 10-16, 1997

Student Analysis

June 10
The completed order for custom fencing (**JOB21**) was delivered to the Ralph E. Maxwell job site. Sales invoice **R2047** lists the sales price for the job at $42,500.00. Received a $10,000 check upon delivery and the balance due on the invoice was charged to Mr. Maxwell's account.

^^

June 10
Purchased direct materials for **JOB22** from River City Steel, Inc. The invoice number for this purchase is **M4388** and all prices are listed at net costs. River City Steel extends net 30 terms.

Stock Number	Quant.	Item Description	Unit Cost	Total
B9620	1,900	5/8 T Wall Tube .049	5.10	$9,690.00
S2250	50	2 x .125 x 20	12.25	612.50
				$10,302.50

^^

June 10
Received a certified check for $6,250.00 from Lakeside Pools, Inc. as payment in full on their account. The balance due on the Lakeside account was written off as uncollectible on May 2 of this year after all attempts for collection had failed. Remember that Ramblewood Manufacturing, Inc. uses the direct write-off method (**two entries required**). At the invoice prompt type **RECOV** for recovery of the cash.

^^

June 11
Sold 5,500 shares of Gold Run Corporation common stock that had been held as a short-term investment. The stock sold for 4 1/2, less a sales commission of $224.50. The stock was originally purchased at a total cost of $18,925.50. At the item prompt type **INVST** for investment.

TRANSACTIONS FOR THE WEEK OF JUNE 10-16, 1997

Student Analysis

June 11
Purchased additional direct materials for **JOB22** from Yamasaki Steel, Inc. (invoice **Y1381**). Yamasaki Steel extends 2/10, n/30 credit terms and all prices are shown at net amounts.

Stock Number	Quant.	Item Description	Unit Cost	Total
H4000	50	4 In Sq. Tubing .125	59.00	$2,950.00
G3000	100	3 In Sq. Tubing .095	51.50	5,150.00
				$8,100.00

^^

June 12
Sold old office equipment for $275 cash. The equipment originally cost $950 and depreciation to March 31 of this year (the end of the quarter) totals $825. The asset depreciates on a straight-line basis at a rate of $25 per month and depreciation is calculated to the nearest month (**two entries required**). At the item prompt type **ASALE** for asset sale.

^^

June 12
Issued a debit memo and returned office supplies with a total cost of $15.35 (sales tax included) to Granite Business Supply. The office supplies were purchased on credit June 4 (invoice number **GB447**).

^^

June 12
Discovered that check **10546** issued for $32.55 on June 1 had been recorded in error for $23.55 **and** that the Miscellaneous Expense account had been debited in error for the purchase of office supplies (invoice **22331**). At the item prompt and the check prompt enter **ERROR.**

***TWO ENTRIES ARE REQUIRED FOR ALL JOURNAL ENTRY CORRECTIONS*. Check page 28 for error correction procedures.**

TRANSACTIONS FOR THE WEEK OF JUNE 10-16, 1997

Student Analysis

June 12
Issued check number **10554** for **$16,256** to Golden Welding Supply as payment in full of the accounts payable balance (invoice **G3288**) that is due today.

^^^

June 13
Received a check for $15,500 from Adams Construction Company as an advance payment on a custom fencing job for their newest development (**JOB23**). Since delivery of orders are made in 30 days or less, advance payments are credited directly to the Accounts Receivable account. If the order has not been filled by the end of the accounting period, the advance payment is transferred to the Unearned Revenue account. At the invoice prompt enter **ADVAN** for advance payment.

^^^

June 13
Purchased direct materials for **JOB23,** on account (invoice number **A4466**) from Ambrosini Steel, Inc. All items purchased are shown on the Ambrosini Steel invoice at list prices. **Each item as well as the total of the invoice must be converted to a NET price to be entered correctly in the Ramblewood accounting system.** Remember that Ramblewood records all material purchases at **NET**, and assumes that every discount offered will automatically be earned by payment of the invoice within the discount period. Ambrosini Steel, Inc., offers terms of **1/10, n/30**, and the materials are delivered FOB destination.

Stock Number	Quant.	Item Description	Unit Cost	Total
G3000	160	3" Square Tubing .095	52.00	$8,320.00
F2000	100	2" Square Tubing .095	38.50	3,850.00
				$12,170.00

TRANSACTIONS FOR THE WEEK OF JUNE 10-16, 1997

Student Analysis

June 13
Discounted the June 2, $32,000, 12%, 60-day note receivable. The discount rate charged by the lender is 12%. Be sure to use the 360-day banker's year in your calculations and if necessary, **round the discount to the nearest cent.** At the item prompt type **DISNT** for discounted note.

^^

June 14
Instead of a costly "patch up" repair of the heavy duty bending machine at an estimated cost of $2,860, and charging this cost to an operating expense account, the machine is rebuilt. The cost of this *major overhaul* is $6,540.00 (invoice **U6321**) and is paid in full with check number **10555.** This **extraordinary repair** will **extend the useful life** of the machine to four years.

^^

June 14
Issued check **10556** to Granite Business Supply as payment in full for invoice **GB447** of June 4. In computing the balance due be sure to deduct the amount of the June 12 debit memo for returned office supplies.

^^

June 14
Issued check number **10557** to the Loomis Legal Group for $430 as payment in full on account for legal services received (invoice **L2121**).

TRANSACTIONS FOR THE WEEK OF JUNE 10-16, 1997

Student Analysis

June 15
Received notice from the bank that the $10,000 check, received from Ralph E. Maxwell on June 10 as a down payment on the **JOB21** sale, had not cleared for lack of funds. The balance of this NSF check and an additional $20 fee charged by the bank will be charged back to the Ralph E. Maxwell account. At the invoice prompt type **BADCK** for bad check.

^^

June 15
Purchased indirect materials from Golden Welding Supply (invoice **G3499**). Credit terms from Golden Welding Supply are net 30. At the overhead prompt enter **INMAT**.

Stock Number	Quant.	Item Description	Unit Cost	Total
IM053	2	MSA Acetylene	23.52	47.04
IM088	1	Brazing Rod 1/8, 5#	16.50	16.50
IM041	1	280 Oxygen	24.50	24.50
				$88.04

^^

June 15
Factory salaries for the first June payroll include the following unrecorded factory hours through June 15. Unrecorded hours are for **JOB22** and **JOB23**. All other jobs with activity during this pay period have been completed, transferred, and sold.

Direct Labor charges are entered directly on each job card. Press **F4**, enter the **date**, and select **JOB22**.

Time Tickets for JOB22:
Time ticket **TT458** totals 15.00 hours of welding time @ $55.00 per hour.

Time ticket **TT459** totals 7.5 hours (07.50) of cutting and finishing time @ $44.00 per hour.

Time ticket information continued on page 38

TRANSACTIONS FOR THE WEEK OF JUNE 10-16, 1997

Student Analysis

Time ticket information continued:

Enter the information for each time ticket as instructed by the program. **JOB22** has not yet been completed and **will not be transferred or sold at this time.** Press Q (Quit) to exit **JOB22** and return to the job card menu.

From the job card menu select **JOB23** and enter the labor hours from time tickets **TT460** and **TT461**.

Time Tickets for JOB23:
Time ticket **TT460** totals 10.00 hours of welding time @ $55.00 per hour.

Time ticket **TT461** totals 2.5 hours of cutting and finishing time @ $44.00 per hour.

JOB23 has not yet been completed and **will not be transferred or sold at this time.** Press Q (Quit) to exit **JOB23** and Q again to exit the job card menu and return to the General Journal.

^^^

June 15
Salaries and wages for each area of operation must be recorded for the first half of June. **Three separate entries are required!**

1. Direct labor for June 1-15 totals $4,466.00 and is charged to the Raw and In-Process Inventory account. At the item prompt enter **DRLAB**.

2. Office salaries and wages total $2,888.65 (enter **OFSAL** at the prompt).

3. Indirect labor (**INLAB**) totaling $1,255 is charged to Manufacturing Overhead. The payroll checks will be issued on June 19.

TRANSACTIONS FOR THE WEEK OF JUNE 10-16, 1997

Student Analysis

June 16
Purchased additional direct materials on account (invoice number **A4498**) from Ambrosini Steel. These materials will be used to further the completion of **JOB23**. All items purchased are listed below at **net amounts**. Ambrosini Steel offers credit terms of 1/10, n/30, and the materials are delivered FOB destination.

Stock Number	Quant.	Item Description	Unit Cost	Total
E0150	200	1 1/2" T Wall Tube .065	14.00	$2,800.00
C0750	2,400	3/4" T Wall Tube .065	6.80	16,320.00
				$19,120.00

^^

When all of the transactions for the week of June 10-16 have been entered, call the Trial Balance to the screen and carefully compare your totals to those in the **"Check It Out"** block on page 40. If any of the figures do not match the **"Check It Out"** block, you must carefully analyze all of your journal entries for the week, locate the error/s, and make the necessary corrections. To efficiently complete this analysis and correction procedure, it is recommended that you print a copy of the Trial Balance and a copy of the transactions you have entered. From the main menu select the **General Ledger** option and print the June 16 Trial Balance. Return to the main menu, select the **General Journal** option and print the transactions for the second week, June 10-16. Be sure to use the **error correction procedures** outlined on **pages 28** and **29.**

"CHECK IT OUT"

101 Cash	$106,577.68
105 Accounts Receivable	72,720.00
115 Raw and In-Process Inventory	49,265.00
129 Office Supplies	1,805.45
132 Accumulated Depre., Office Equipment	15,695.00
136 Accumulated Deprec., Shop Equipment	19,165.00
185 Manufacturing Overhead	1,892.58
201 Accounts Payable	125,057.88
209 Salaries & Wages Payable	8,609.65
221 Unearned Revenue	0.00
401 Custom Fencing and Gate Sales	278,412.00
501 Cost of Goods Sold	191,691.30
623 Bad Debt Expense	1,250.65
721 Gain on Sale of Assets	327.00
731 Gain on Short-Term Investments	6,401.00
741 Miscellaneous Revenue	521.00
813 Interest Expense	576.40
TRIAL BALANCE	$805,201.22

CHECK THE JOB CARDS

1. Return to the main menu and select the **Subsidiary Ledger** option. From the sub menu select (J), the **Job Cost Ledger** option and select (J) for **Single Job Card**.

2. Select **JOB22** and display the job card on the screen. The totals to-date on the **JOB22** job card should show:

   A. **$18,402.50 for direct materials**
   B. **$ 1,155.00 for direct labor**
   C. **$ 924.00 for manufacturing overhead**
   D. **Total costs as of June 16, $20,481.50**

   Press any key to continue and return to the job card menu.

3. Select **JOB23** and display the job card on the screen. **JOB23** is in process and on June 16 has total costs to-date of **$32,356.30.**

IF ALL OF YOUR TOTALS MATCH THE CHECK FIGURES and JOB CARDS, you are ready to print selected documents and use them to answer the Mid-Point Evaluation questions.

PLEASE NOTE: ALL OF THE JUNE 16 DOCUMENTS MUST BE PRINTED BEFORE CONTINUING THE JOURNALIZING PROCESS FOR JUNE 17-23. THE TRIAL BALANCE, AND SCHEDULES CANNOT BE PRINTED FOR JUNE 16 IF ENTRIES AFTER JUNE 16 HAVE BEEN JOURNALIZED!

When your totals match the check figures and the job card totals, print the following documents:

1. **Trial Balance for June 16, 1997** *(Select the General Ledger option from the Main Menu. The Trial Balance is an option on the General Ledger sub menu.)*

2. **General Ledger accounts for:**

   101 Cash
   105 Accounts Receivable
   115 Raw and In-Process Inventory
   185 Manufacturing Overhead
   201 Accounts Payable
   401 Custom Fencing and Gate Sales
   501 Cost of Goods Sold

3. **The Schedule of Accounts Receivable**

   A. Select Subsidiary Ledgers from the Main Menu
   B. Select Accounts Receivable and Accounts Payable
   C. Select Accounts Receivable Ledger
   D. Select Schedule of Accounts Receivable
   E. Select the Date (June 16)
   F. Select Print the Schedule
   G. Print the Schedule

4. **Entire Subsidiary Ledger for all customers**

5. **The Schedule of Accounts Payable**

6. **Entire Subsidiary Ledger for all creditors/vendors**

7. Job Cards

A. Select Subsidiary Ledgers from the Main Menu
B. Select the Job Cost Ledger from the Sub Menu
C. Print All Job Cards

8. Schedule of Job Cards

A. Select the Job Cost Ledger from the Sub Menu
B. Print the Schedule of Job Cards

Using the printed documents, answer the questions on the Mid-Project Evaluation forms.

BE SURE TO PRINT ALL OF YOUR DOCUMENTS BEFORE CONTINUING THE JOURNALIZING PROCESS FOR JUNE 17-23!

MID-PROJECT EVALUATION

RAMBLEWOOD MANUFACTURING, INCORPORATED

June 16, 1997

MID-PROJECT EVALUATION **NAME**____________________

RAMBLEWOOD MANUFACTURING, INC. **SECTION**______**DATE**__________

1. Do the totals on your printed Trial Balance match the figures shown in the "**Check It Out**" block? **YES**______**NO**______

2. What was the correct balance of the Cash account at the close of business on June 5? **$**____________

3. What invoice was paid in full with check number 10552 on June 4? **Invoice Number**____________

4-5. Which customer paid invoice number R2020 in full and on what date was the invoice paid? **Customer Number**____________

Date____________

6. What was the correct balance of the Accounts Receivable account at the close of business on June 10? **$**____________

7-8. An entry for $10,250.00 was debited to the Accounts Receivable account on June 7. Which customer made this charge and what is the sales invoice number? **Customer Number**____________

Sales Invoice Number____________

9. Adams Construction Company has a negative balance (-$15,500) listed on the Schedule of Accounts Receivable. What is the reason for this negative balance? ____________________

10. Why does the Fontaine Storage account now have a $0.00 balance? ____________

11. Does the balance of the Schedule of Accounts Receivable match the balance of the Accounts Receivable account? **YES**______**NO**______

12. Does the balance of the Schedule of Accounts Payable match the balance of the Accounts Payable account? **YES**______**NO**______

13. By what date must the next payment on account be made to Klondyke Air and Gas (assume every discount is taken)? **Date**____________

14. What was the balance of the Yamasaki Steel, Inc. account after the purchase of direct materials on June 9? **$**____________

15. Examine **carefully** the Yamasaki Steel, Inc., acccount. What problem can you identify with this account at this time? ____________________

16. Assuming that all cash discounts are taken, on what date is the next accounts payable invoice balance owed to Ambrosini Steel, Inc., due and payable? **Date**____________

MID-PROJECT EVALUATION
RAMBLEWOOD MANUFACTURING, INC.

17. If the balance of the June 16 invoice (A4498) from Ambrosini Steel, Inc. is not paid on or before June 26, what will be the cost of failing to take the discount? Remember that the balance owed is a net amount. $____________

18. What terms are extended by the Loomis Legal Group? ____________

19. How many of the current outstanding invoices for River City Steel, Inc., must be paid before June 30? ____________

20. Analyze the Accounts Payable Ledger and determine the number of the next invoice to be paid that will result in savings from paying in time to qualify for the discount. **Invoice Number**____________

Use the individual job cards and the schedule of Raw and In-Process Job Cards to answer the following questions.

21. How many jobs have been completed and sold in June? ____________

22. What is the total cost of jobs in process as of June 16? $____________

Examine Job Card JOB19 to answer questions 23-29:

23. On what date was this job started? **Date**____________

24. On what date was this job completed? **Date**____________

25. How many hours were charged to this job for cutting and finishing? (Welding @ $50 per hour, and Cutting & Finishing @ $30 per hour were the hourly labor charges prior to June 1.) ____________

26. Twelve hours of cutting and finishing was reported on what time ticket? **Number**____________

27. On what date was JOB19 sold? **Date**____________

28. What was the sales invoice number for the sale of JOB19? **Number**____________

29. What was the cost for direct labor on JOB19? $____________

Examine Job Card JOB20 to answer questions 30-35:

30. What was the manufacturing overhead cost on JOB20? $____________

Round all percentage answers to two decimal places: 23.57689 = 23.58

31. Direct labor is what percent of the total cost of JOB20? ____________%

32. How many total hours of labor were charged to JOB20? ____________

MID-PROJECT EVALUATION
RAMBLEWOOD MANUFACTURING, INC.

33. During May what were the two rates charged for labor on JOB20? $________ & $________

34. The labor rates for cutting and finishing increased by what percent on June 1? ________%

35. If time ticket TT455 had charged 12 hours for the finishing work on June 7 instead of the 6 hours reported, what would have been the total charge for manufacturing overhead? (Overhead is charged at 80% of direct labor costs.) $________

Examine Job Card JOB21 to answer questions 36-40:

36. JOB21 was originally budgeted for $29,288. By what amount did the completed cost of the job exceed the budgeted price? $________

37. JOB21 was completed at what percent over the budgeted price? ________%

38. What percent of the total cost of JOB21 is for direct materials? ________%

39. What percent of the total cost of JOB21 is for direct labor? ________%

40. Which vendor (identify by name) supplied the $951.50 in materials that were purchased for JOB21 on June 7? ________

RAMBLEWOOD MANUFACTURING, INCORPORATED

TRANSACTIONS

FOR

JUNE 17 - 23

TRANSACTIONS FOR THE WEEK OF JUNE 17-23, 1997

Student Analysis

June 17
A careful examination of the accounts payable shows that the June 2 invoice (number **Y1295**) from Yamasaki Steel, Inc., was filed incorrectly and the 2% discount has been lost. Record the required entry to account for this error. This invoice will be paid in full (list price) on July 2 (net 30).

^^

June 17
Issued check **10558** for $951.50 to Delta Supply as payment in full for the June 7 invoice (**D4689**) that is due today.

^^

June 17
Purchased direct raw materials on account (invoice number **M4484**) from River City Steel, Inc. **Net 30** terms are provided by River City Steel and the materials are delivered FOB destination. The materials are for **JOB24**, a special replacement and repair job for customer Samuel Fuller.

Stock Number	Quant.	Item Description	Unit Cost	Total
A5000	20	1/2" T Wall Tube .049	3.50	$ 70.00
C0750	100	3/4" T Wall Tube .065	6.80	680.00
				$750.00

^^

June 17
Issued check **10559** for $12,462.70 to River City Steel as payment in full of the May 18 invoice (**M3910**) that is due today.

TRANSACTIONS FOR THE WEEK OF JUNE 17-23, 1997

Student Analysis

June 18
Received a cashiers check for $10,020 and a letter of apology from customer Ralph E. Maxwell. The check is to cover a NSF check that was received as a partial payment June 10 for JOB21. At the invoice prompt enter **RECOV** for recovery.

^^^

June 18
Issued check number **10560** to the Gold River State Bank to cover the payroll (**PAYRL**) for the first half of June that will be issued through this bank account on June 19. Check the June 15 payroll entries for the amount needed to cover the payroll checks.

^^^

June 18
Purchased direct raw materials on account (invoice number **M4512**) from River City Steel, Inc. The additional materials are for continuing work on **JOB23**. All items are purchased under **net 30** terms and are delivered FOB destination.

Stock Number	Quant.	Item Description	Unit Cost	Total
G3000	152	3" Square Tubing .095	44.55	$6,771.60
E0150	240	1 1/2" T Wall Tube .065	14.00	3,360.00
C0750	1,150	3/4" T Wall Tube .065	6.80	7,820.00
				$17,951.60

^^^

June 19
Issued check number **10561** to Ace Credit Services as payment in full on the $36,000, 12%, 90-day, note payable that is due today. At the invoice prompt enter **NTPAY** for note payable.

TRANSACTIONS FOR THE WEEK OF JUNE 17-23, 1997

Student Analysis

June 19
Purchased indirect materials on account (invoice number **K1440**) from Klondyke Air & Gas. All items purchased are listed below at **net amounts.** Klondyke extends terms of 2/15, n/30, and goods are delivered FOB destination. At the overhead prompt enter **INMAT**.

Stock Number	Quant.	Item Description	Unit Cost	Total
IM041	20	280 Oxygen	24.50	$490.00
IM053	25	MSA Acetylene	23.52	588.00
				$1,078.00

^^

June 19
Issued check **10562** for $2,346.00 to Yamasaki Steel, Inc., as payment in full for invoice **Y1332** that is due today.

^^

June 20
Final time tickets have been completed for **JOB22**. Press the **F4 key**, enter the **date**, select job card **JOB22**, and enter the labor hours reported.

Time ticket **TT462** reports **22** hours of welding time @ **$55.00** per hour.

Time ticket **TT463** reports **15** hours and **30** minutes (15.50 hours) of finishing time @ **$44.00** per hour.

Direct Labor charges are entered directly on each job card.

JOB22 is now finished and ready to be delivered to the customer. Write the total cost of the completed job here! $____________ This total will be used for the next journal entry.

TRANSACTIONS FOR THE WEEK OF JUNE 17-23, 1997

Student Analysis

June 20
Record the transfer of the completed fencing for **JOB22** out of Raw and In-Process Inventory.

^^^

June 20
Issued check **10563** for $353.50 to Klondyke Air & Gas as payment in full of invoice **K1244** that is due today.

^^^

June 20
Delivered the custom fencing (**JOB22**) to the job site for Wasaki Pool and Spa. Sales invoice **R2048** lists the sales price for the job at $34,000. The full amount of the sale was charged to the customer's account.

^^^

June 21
Purchased additional direct materials for **JOB23** from Ambrosini Steel, Inc. Invoice **A4555** itemizes the materials at **list prices.** Be sure to convert the total invoice cost to a **net** amount when recording the journal entry. The credit terms offered by Ambrosini Steel, Inc., are 2/15, n/30.

Stock Number	Quant.	Item Description	Unit Cost	Total
D0199	200	1" Solid	35.00	$7,000.00
XX105	1	Electronic Gate Set	600.00	600.00
				$7,600.00

TRANSACTIONS FOR THE WEEK OF JUNE 17-23, 1997

Student Analysis

June 21
Issued check **10564** for $8,100.00 to Yamasaki Steel, Inc., as payment in full of invoice **Y1381** that is due today.

^^

June 21
Issued check number **10565** for $86.44 and purchased additional factory tools (invoice number **11110**) to be used in the cutting and finishing process. The cost of the tools is charged to the Manufacturing Overhead account. At the overhead prompt enter **TOOLS.**

^^

June 21
Additional welding and cutting work has been completed on **JOB23.** Press the **F4 key,** enter the **date**, select job card **JOB23,** and enter the labor hours.

Time ticket **TT464** reports **13.50** hours of welding time @ **$55.00** per hour.

Time ticket **TT465** reports **19.00** hours of cutting time @ **$44.00** per hour.

JOB23 has not yet been completed at this time.

^^

June 21
Issued check **10566** and purchased new office equipment. The office equipment lists for $1,375.00 with **trade discounts of 40%** and **5%**. The invoice number for this purchase is **Z8000.**

TRANSACTIONS FOR THE WEEK OF JUNE 17-23, 1997

Student Analysis

June 22
Traded the old delivery truck for a new truck issuing check number **10567** to complete the transaction. The old truck cost $3,600 and on March 31, the end of the quarter, had depreciated $2,350. Straight-line depreciation on the old truck is **$50 per month**. The new truck listed for $12,500 (invoice **M1212**) and Folsom Auto Sales allowed a $2,800 trade-in allowance on the purchase of the new vehicle. At the item prompt enter **DEPRE.** **Two entries are required to properly record this trade.**

^^

June 22
A check (number **10568**) for $328.00 was issued to the Department of Motor Vehicles (invoice **DMV06**) for the vehicle license and registration fees.

^^

June 22
Received notice from the bank that the discounted note receivable from Berline, Incorporated, had been dishonored as of the close of the work day June 21. The bank charged the Ramblewood cash account a total of $10,225 which included a $25 protest fee for handling. The $10,000, 12%, 60-day note was received on April 22 as payment in full on sales invoice **R2001**. The note was discounted the same day to provide cash for current liability obligations. Charge this note back to the Berline, Incorporated, account. At the invoice prompt type **DISHO** for dishonored note.

^^

June 23
Issued check **10569** and purchased factory supplies **(FSUPP)** from Auburn Supply. Invoice number **A1490** lists the net cost of the supplies at $145.00. These supplies are used in the manufacturing process.

TRANSACTIONS FOR THE WEEK OF JUNE 17-23, 1997

Student Analysis

June 23
Time tickets for **JOB24** have been completed. Time ticket **TT466** totals **2.5** hours of welding time @ **$55.00** per hour.

Time ticket **TT467** totals **5.0** hours of cutting and finishing time @ **$44.00** per hour.

JOB24 is now completed. The total cost of the completed job is $__________.

^^^

June 23
Record the transfer of the completed fencing and accessories for **JOB24** out of Raw and In-Process Inventory. **JOB24 has been completed and will be delivered to the customer (sold) later.**

^^^

June 23
Borrowed $48,000 cash by issuing a 60-day discounted note payable to a private lender. The lender charges a 12% discount fee. Remember that the 360-day banker's year is used in calculating interest. Because of the timing of this note, the lender discount will be debited to the Discount on Notes Payable account. At the item prompt enter **NTPAY** for note payable.

^^^

When all of the transactions for the week have been entered, call the trial balance to the screen and check your account totals against the figures in the **"Check It Out"** block.

Select the Subsidiary Ledger option and print a copy of the Schedule of Job Cards. **JOB24** has just been completed but has not yet been sold, and **JOB23** is still in process on June 23. The schedule total for these jobs is **$60,597.20**.

If all of your totals match the check figures, you are ready to enter the transactions for the period of June 24-30. If your totals do not match the check figures, carefully check the journal entries, locate the error/s, and enter the necessary correction/s. **Remember the most efficient way to locate errors is to print a copy of the General Journal and the Trial Balance! For the job cards, carefully check the accuracy of the material and labor entries and amounts that have been recorded this week.**

"CHECK IT OUT"

101 Cash	$ 72,466.14
105 Accounts Receivable	106,925.00
115 Raw and In-Process Materials	50,134.00
131 Office Equipment	33,169.25
139 Trucks	52,800.00
140 Accumulated Depreciation, Trucks	2,170.00
185 Manufacturing Overhead	3,202.02
201 Accounts Payable	128,361.78
203 Notes Payable	48,000.00
209 Salaries & Wages Payable	0.00
401 Custom Fencing and Gate Sales	312,412.00
501 Cost of Goods Sold	216,971.90
628 License Expense	579.00
813 Interest Expense	1,656.40
814 Discounts Lost	527.15
TRIAL BALANCE	$843,545.47

RAMBLEWOOD MANUFACTURING, INCORPORATED

T R A N S A C T I O N S

F O R

J U N E 24 - 30

TRANSACTIONS FOR THE WEEK OF JUNE 24-30, 1997

Student Analysis

June 24
Received a $14,000, 15%, 60-day, note receivable from customer Ralph E. Maxwell as payment in full on invoice **R2038** of May 25.

^^

June 24
Issued check **10570** for $12,048.30 to Ambrosini Steel, Inc., as payment in full on purchase invoice number **A4466** dated June 13. Ambrosini Steel allows a five-day grace period for late payments. The discount will not be lost with this payment being one day late.

^^

June 25
Received a check for $7,500 from Sierra College as a deposit on a custom fencing project for the parking lot and the new day care center (**JOB25**). At the invoice prompt enter (**ADVAN**).

^^

June 25
Sold and delivered special order **JOB24** to customer Samuel Fuller. This job was completed and transferred out of the Raw and In-Process Materials account on June 23. Mr. Fuller paid the $1,975.00 total of sales invoice **R2049** with a bank credit card. All bank card sales are the same as cash and all credit card fees are accounted for at the end of the month.

^^

June 25
Issued check **10571** for $15,500 to Svenson's Mechanical of Alameda for leasehold improvements made to the hoist, storage, and receiving areas. The invoice number from Svenson's is **SV303.**

TRANSACTIONS FOR THE WEEK OF JUNE 24-30, 1997

Student Analysis

June 25
Purchased direct materials on account from River City Steel to start **JOB25** for Sierra College. Terms are net 30 and the materials are delivered to the Ramblewood factory **(M4595)**.

Stock Number	Quant.	Item Description	Unit Cost	Total
F2000	500	2" Square Tubing .095	29.00	$14,500.00
XX105	1	Electronic Gate	588.00	588.00
H4000	100	4" Square Tubing .125	62.00	6,200.00
				$21,288.00

^^^

June 26
Traded an old forklift (shop equipment) for a newer model issuing check number **10572** to complete the transaction. The old forklift cost $4,950 and on May 31, had depreciated $2,600. Units-of-production depreciation (**DEPRE**) is used for the forklift and 25 cents per hour is the depreciation rate. The hour meter shows 106.0 hours of use since the end of last month. The newer forklift lists for $9,800 (invoice **13355**) and a $3,200 trade-in allowance on the old forklift is given by the seller. The IRS method is used for recording all trades. **Two entries are required** with one entry debiting **Manufacturing Overhead.**

^^^

June 26
Sold old office equipment at a parking lot sale for $150.00. The office equipment cost $950.00 and was fully depreciated at the time of the sale. At the item prompt enter **ASALE** for asset sale.

^^^

June 26
Issued check **10573** for $19,120.00 to Ambrosini Steel, Inc., as payment in full on purchase invoice **A4498** of June 16.

TRANSACTIONS FOR THE WEEK OF JUNE 24-30, 1997

Student Analysis

June 27
Received a check from Berline, Incorporated for $10,245.45 as payment in full on their dishonored note of **June 22** and **12% interest** from the **June 21 due date** to June 27. At the invoice prompt enter **DISNT** for dishonored note.

^^^

June 27
Issued the following checks as payment in full for miscellaneous billings:

> Check **10574** to Mountain Services for truck gas and repairs totaling $545.80 (invoice **44555**). The truck **is used for delivery only.**
>
> Check **10575** for $260.00 to Sierra Accountancy, Inc., for accounting services (invoice **S2546**).
>
> Check **10576** for $1,200.00 to Placer Homes magazine for business advertising (invoice number **W5000**).

^^^

June 27
Additional welding and cutting work has been completed on **JOB23**. Press the **F4 key,** enter the **date**, select job card **JOB23**, and enter the labor hours.

Time ticket **TT468** reports **10.50** hours of welding time @ **$55.00** per hour.

Time Ticket **TT469** reports **05.25** hours of cutting time @ **$44.00** per hour.

JOB23 has not yet been completed at this time.

^^^

June 28
Major repairs costing $796.00 were made on the used forklift that was purchased on June 26. These repairs were necessary **before the vehicle could be placed in service.** Issued check **10577** as payment is full for invoice number **Z7777**.

TRANSACTIONS FOR THE WEEK OF JUNE 24-30, 1997

Student Analysis

June 28
Utilities (electric and gas) totaling $535.50 are paid in full with check number **10578** (invoice **15666**). Utility costs are prorated with **90%** allocated to the manufacturing process and **10%** to administration. Telephone billings (prorated at **20%** for the manufacturing process and **80%** for administration) totaling $466.70 are paid in full with check number **10579** (invoice **2555T**). **Two entries are required. Use an appropriate five-character code (UTILI or PHONE) at the overhead prompt.**

^^

June 29
Purchased the final portion of direct materials for **JOB23** from Ambrosini Steel, Inc. Invoice **A4600** itemizes the materials at **list prices**. Convert the total invoice cost to a **net** amount when recording the journal entry. The credit terms offered by Ambrosini Steel, Inc., are 2/15, n/30.

Stock Number	Quant.	Item Description	Unit Cost	Total
D0199	50	1" Solid	35.00	$1,750.00
D0085	10	2" Solid	70.00	700.00
				$2,450.00

^^

June 29
Rent has been paid for six months in advance under a long-term rental agreement with the landlord. Monthly rent totals $3,250 and is allocated to the factory area and office area on the basis of space utilization. A total of **85%** of the rented area is used for production work and **15%** for office and administrative services. Enter **RENTS** at the overhead prompt. ***Remember that items that are charged to the Manufacturing Overhead account are updated monthly.***

TRANSACTIONS FOR THE WEEK OF JUNE 24-30, 1997

Student Analysis

June 30
Exactly five years remain on the leasehold agreement on May 31, 1997 and the unamortized balance of the **Leasehold** account is $45,000. The ***monthly*** amortization of this account is recorded using the same percentages as the rent allocation (June 29 entry). Enter **LEASE** at the overhead prompt.

^^^

June 30
The May 31, 1997 balance of the **Leasehold Improvements** account is $48,000. The improvements are amortized over the same period as the leasehold and **all** leasehold improvements made to the property have been made to the **factory production and manufacturing area.** Record the monthly leasehold improvements amortization entry **(LEIMP).**

^^

June 30

Three entries required:

Expired insurance on **shop assets and the manufacturing sector** of Ramblewood Manufacturing totals $680 for the month **(INSUR).**

Accrued property taxes on **factory assets** for the month ended June 30, 1997 total $155 **(PRTAX).**

Depreciation not yet recorded on **shop equipment** totals $703.50 for the month **(DEPRE).**

^^

June 30
An analysis of the Accounts Payable accounts reveals the June 8 invoice **(K1299)** from Klondyke Air & Gas (list price of $98.00, terms of 2/10, n/30) should have been paid by June 18 to take advantage of the 2% cash discount offered. **The lost discount must be recognized at this time.** The full amount of the invoice will be paid on or before July 8.

TRANSACTIONS FOR THE WEEK OF JUNE 24-30, 1997

Student Analysis

June 30

One year ago on June 30, 1996 a capital lease for shop equipment was signed with Sacramento Equipment Company. The agreement called for sixteen quarterly lease payments of $500 to be paid the last working day of each quarter for the next four years. On the date the contract was signed the prevailing interest rate was 10% and the journal entry included debits to Shop Equipment for $6,527.50 and Discount On Lease Financing for $1,472.50. The equipment will become the property of the lessee at the end of the lease period. The **interest method** is used to amortize the Discount on Lease Financing and the amount to be amortized for the quarter totals $137.29. The chart below presents the results of the interest calculations for the first six quarters.

The equipment depreciates on a straight-line basis, has a salvage value of $1,727.50, and an estimated life of five years.

Three entries are required.

1. Issue check **10580** for the quarterly lease payment. At the invoice prompt enter **LEASE.**

2. Amortize the Discount on Lease Financing for the quarter. At the item prompt enter **AMORT.**

3. Record the **monthly depreciation** for the "leased to own" shop equipment **(charge to Manufacturing Overhead).** Remember that Items charged to Manufacturing Overhead are updated monthly. At the overhead prompt enter **DEPRE.**

Lease Payment per Quarter	**$500.00**
Term of Lease in Quarters	**16**
Prevailing Annual Interest Rate	**10.00%**

Time Period	Beginning Of Quarter Lease Liability	Beginning Of Quarter Unamortized Discount	Beginning Of Quarter Carrying Amount	Discount To Be Amortized	End Of Quarter Lease Liability	End Of Quarter Unamortized Discount	End Of Quarter Carrying Amount
1	$8,000.00	$1,472.50	$6,527.50	$163.19	$7,500.00	$1,309.31	$6,190.69
2	7,500.00	1,309.31	6,190.69	154.77	7,000.00	1,154.54	5,845.46
3	7,000.00	1,154.54	5,845.46	146.14	6,500.00	1,008.41	5,491.59
4	6,500.00	1,008.41	5,491.59	137.29	6,000.00	871.12	5,128.88
5	6,000.00	871.12	5,128.88	128.22	5,500.00	742.90	4,757.10
6	5,500.00	742.90	4,757.10	118.93	5,000.00	623.97	4,376.03

TRANSACTIONS FOR THE WEEK OF JUNE 24-30, 1997

Student Analysis

June 30
Factory salaries for the second June payroll include the following unrecorded factory labor hours through June 30. The unrecorded hours are for **JOB23** and **JOB25**, **both of which are in process** and **will not be completed and transferred this quarter**. All other jobs with activity during this pay period have been completed and sold.

Press the **F4 key,** enter the **date**, select job card **JOB23**, and enter the labor hours.

Time ticket **TT470** reports **12.50** hours of finishing time @ **$44.00** per hour.

Press **Q** to Quit and exit **JOB23**.

Select **JOB25** and enter the labor hours.

Time ticket **TT471** reports **32.25** hours of welding time @ **$55.00** per hour.

Time Ticket **TT472** reports **15.75** hours of cutting time @ **$44.00** per hour.

Exit the job card, the job card menu, and return to the general journal. **JOB23 and JOB25 are scheduled to be completed in July.**

^^^

June 30
Salaries and wages for the second half of June must be recorded for each area of operation. Payroll checks will be issued on July 3. **Three separate entries are required.**

1. Office salaries and wages for the second half of June total $2,856.56. At the item prompt enter **OFSAL**.

2. Direct labor (**DRLAB**) for the period totals $7,653.25 and is charged to the Raw and In-Process Inventory account. At the item prompt enter **DRLAB**.

3. Indirect labor (**INLAB**) totaling $2,665.65 is charged to Manufacturing Overhead.

TRANSACTIONS FOR THE WEEK OF JUNE 24-30, 1997

Student Analysis

June 30
JOB23, started June 13 for Adams Construction Company, has not been completed as of June 30 (the end of the quarter). The $15,500.00 cash advance, which was received and credited to the Accounts Receivable account, is **unearned** and must be transferred to the Unearned Revenue account (enter **ADVAN** at the invoice prompt).

^^

June 30
JOB25, started June 25 for Sierra College, has not been completed this week (the end of the quarter). The $7,500.00 cash advance (**ADVAN**), received and credited to the Accounts Receivable account, is **unearned** and must be transferred to the Unearned Revenue account.

^^

June 30

Only one credit card charge of $1,975 was made by a customer during the month of June. The bank credit card expense is 4% of the total amount of the charge. A monthly statement received from the bank has charged this fee against the cash account. At the check number prompt enter **BKFEE** for bank fees. At the invoice prompt enter **CCARD** for credit cards.

^^

June 30
Manufacturing Overhead for the month is applied (**APPLY**) at 80% of the direct labor cost. The total direct labor cost for the month of June totals $12,119.25.

When all of the transactions for the final week have been entered, call the trial balance to the screen and check your account totals against the figures in the **"Check It Out"** block. If your totals do not match the check figures, carefully check the journal entries, locate the error/s, and enter the necessary correction/s. When your totals match the "Check It Out" block, proceed to the **"Final Inventory Check"**. **Remember that the most efficient way to locate errors is to print a copy of the General Journal and the Trial Balance!**

"CHECK IT OUT"

101 Cash	$ 34,685.29
105 Accounts Receivable	98,200.00
109 Notes Receivable	14,000.00
115 Raw and In-Process Inventory	91,171.65
132 Accumulated Depreciation, Office Equipment	14,745.00
135 Shop Equipment	131,684.50
136 Accumulated Depreciation, Shop Equipment	17,348.50
145 Leasehold Improvements	62,700.00
160 Leasehold	44,250.00
185 Manufacturing Overhead	2,592.56
201 Accounts Payable	120,884.44
209 Salaries & Wages Payable	13,175.46
211 Estimated Property Taxes Payable	155.00
221 Unearned Revenues	23,000.00
231 Long-Term Lease Liability	6,000.00
232 Discount On Lease Financing	871.12
401 Custom Fencing and Gate Sales	314,387.00
604 Advertising Expense	3,049.75
607 Credit Card Expense	119.00
621 Rent Expense	1,800.00
625 Electric and Gas Expense	196.55
626 Telephone Expense	485.36
711 Interest Earned	553.33
721 Gain On Sales Of Assets	477.00
813 Interest Expense	1,793.69
814 Discounts Lost	529.11
TRIAL BALANCE	$ 871,277.54

CHECK THE JOB CARDS

From the main menu select the **Subsidiary Ledger** option. From the sub menu select the **Job Cost Ledger** option. The Job Cost Ledger will list **JOB23 and JOB25** as still in process. The June 30 total of the cost of these jobs is **<u>$91,171.65</u>**.

If all of your totals match the check figures, proceed to the **Adjusting Entries For The Quarter** section. If your totals do not match the check figures, **print a trial balance and general journal (job cards if needed).** Carefully check the journal entries, locate the error/s, and record the required correction/s.

RAMBLEWOOD MANUFACTURING INCORPORATED

ADJUSTING AND CLOSING ENTRIES

For the Quarter Ended June 30, 1997

ADJUSTING ENTRIES FOR THE QUARTER

Using a copy of the June 30 Trial Balance and the information and financial data shown below, record the adjusting entries for Ramblewood Manufacturing, Inc. **BE SURE TO USE THE JOURNALIZE ADJUSTING ENTRIES OPTION.** Adjusting entries **must not** be entered using the regular Journalize Daily Entries procedure. Corrections to adjusting entries must also be entered using the **Journalize Adjusting Entries** option. **ALL ENTRIES MUST BE RECORDED AS OF JUNE 30, THE END OF THE SECOND QUARTER!**

A. The office supplies inventory is **$753.22.**

B. The insurance expense applicable to the administrative and office operations portion of the business totals **$425.75.**

C. A total of **$625.00** worth of advertising copy, paid for and **correctly charged** to the Advertising Expense account, will be received next quarter.

D. Accrued property tax on office equipment totals **$188.00.**

E. Accrue the interest on the **short-term** note receivable. **On all financial computations calculate the interest to the nearest cent. Use the 360-day banker's year for all interest computations.**

Note One: $14,000, 15%, 60-day note dated June 24

F. Depreciation of office equipment totals **$1,745.00 for the quarter.**

G. Ramblewood Maufacturing, Inc. has two trucks. The new truck acquired on June 22 will not depreciate this quarter. The truck used for business travel and delivery was acquired late last year at a cost of $42,000. The vehicle has an estimated salvage value of $12,000, an estimated service life of 150,000 miles, and is depreciated on a miles-driven basis (units of production). The vehicle was driven a total of **5,185** miles during the quarter.

H. On June 23, $48,000 cash was borrowed on a 60-day discounted note and $960 was debited to the Discount On Notes Payable account (12% discount fee).

I. Additional income tax expense for the period totals **$1,856.00**.

When all of the adjusting entries have been correctly entered, PRINT THE ADJUSTED TRIAL BALANCE! The correct balance will be $876,138.54.

You are now ready to complete the final evaluation of the Ramblewood Manufacturing, Inc. operations. **To gather the necessary documentation to complete the final evaluation questions, PRINT ALL of the documents listed in instructions 1-7.**

1. **Income Statement, Statement of Cost of Goods Manufactured, Cost of Goods Sold, Retained Earnings Statement, and the Balance Sheet**

   THE CORRECT NET INCOME FOR RAMBLEWOOD MANUFACTURING, INCORPORATED IS BETWEEN $62,600.00 AND $62,800.00.

2. **The Schedule of Accounts Receivable** *(Select Subsidiary Ledgers from the Main Menu)*

3. **The entire Accounts Receivable Subsidiary Ledger**

4. **The Schedule of Accounts Payable**

5. **The entire Accounts Payable Subsidiary Ledger**

6. **All Job Cards** *(Select Subsidiary Ledgers from the Main Menu)*

7. **The Schedule of Job Cards**

Record the Closing Entries for Ramblewood Manufacturing, Inc.

The closing process in the Ramblewood Manufacturing, Inc. accounting system is an automatic function. The computer will close all of the temporary accounts and adjust the Merchandise Inventory account. From the **General Journal** sub menu select the **Automatic Closing/Restoring** option. Select (C) to close the accounts. Return to the main menu, select the **General Ledger Menu** option and print the following documents:

1. **General Ledger accounts for:**

101 Cash
105 Accounts Receivable
185 Manufacturing Overhead
201 Accounts Payable
305 Retained Earnings
311 Dividends Declared
501 Cost of Goods Sold
901 Income Summary

2. **Post-Closing Trial Balance**

Exit the Ramblewood Manufacturing, Inc. accounting system. Using all of your printed documents, carefully answer the **Final Evaluation** questions beginning on page 81. The questions and several of the end-of-the-quarter documents may be collected by your instructor.

Error Correction After Closing the Books

If, after closing the books, you discover an error or wish to print a corrected copy of any of the financial statements, you must use the **Automatic Closing/Restoring** option and return the accounts to their pre-closing balances. Select the **R** option and restore the journal and ledgers to pre-closing balances.

BEFORE MAKING ANY CORRECTIONS TO REGULAR OR ADJUSTING ENTRIES, YOU MUST PRINT AN ADJUSTED TRIAL BALANCE. THIS PROCEDURE WILL REESTABLISH YOUR PRE-CLOSING BALANCES FOR ADDITIONAL ADJUSTMENT OR CORRECTION!

Daily or adjusting entries can then be corrected using the **Journalize Daily Entries** or **Journalize Adjusting Entries** option. After any corrections a new Adjusted Trial Balance must be printed as well as corrected copies of all required documents. Again, close the books using the **Automatic Closing/Restoring** procedure, print a corrected **Post-Closing Trial Balance** and any corrected general ledger accounts. Exit the system.

FINAL EVALUATION

RAMBLEWOOD MANUFACTURING INCORPORATED

June 30, 1997

FINAL EVALUATION **NAME**____________________

RAMBLEWOOD MANUFACTURING, INC. **SECTION**______ **DATE**__________

1. How much cash was paid out (checks issued) on June 22? **$**____________

2-3. Check number 10568 was issued to the Department of Motor Vehicles. On what date was this check issued and what was the number of the invoice paid? **Date**____________ **Invoice Number**____________

4-5. What check number paid invoice SV303 and on what date was the check issued? **Check Number**____________ **Date**____________

6. Does Ramblewood Manufacturing, Inc. have enough cash on hand to meet its current liabilities? **YES**______ **NO**______

7. What is the reason for the June 25 debit entry of $7,500 to the Cash Account?

____

8. Over the next three years the balance of the Discount on Lease Financing account will be amortized to what account? ________________

9. What is the Income From Operations for the quarter? **$**____________

10. If more efficient operation of the business had allowed management to reduce cost of goods sold by 1% and operating expenses by 2%, what would be the Net Income for the quarter? **$**____________

Remember that for all percentage questions your answers must be rounded to two decimal positions (4.57689% = 4.58%).

11. Cost of goods sold is what percent of Custom Fencing and Gate Sales? ____________**%**

12. Gross Margin is what percent of Custom Fencing and Gate Sales? ____________**%**

13. Income From Operations is what percent of Custom Fencing and Gate Sales? ____________**%**

14. Last quarter Income From Operations was 21.24% of Custom Fencing and Gate Sales. Is this quarter an improvement over last quarter? **YES**______ **NO**______

15. Ramblewood Manufacturing attempts to bid all projects to be completed and sold at 45% above total costs for each project. Has that objective been reached this quarter? **YES**______ **NO**______

16. Total Operating Expenses are what percent of Custom Fencing and Gate Sales? ____________**%**

17. Last year (for the second quarter ended June 30, 1996) Revenues and the Gross Margin were almost the same as this quarter in actual dollars. However, Income from Operations was $1,500 lower. Explain how this might occur.

____

FINAL EVALUATION
RAMBLEWOOD MANUFACTURING, INC.

18. What percentage of net income can be attributed to the gain on short-term investments (do not adjust for changes due to income taxes)? ____________%

19. Office Salaries and Wages Expense is budgeted at 50% of the total operating expenses. This quarter this expense has exceeded the budgeted amount by what percent? ____________%

20. What is the book value of the Shop Equipment? $____________

21. What is the current ratio? ____________

22. What is the acid-test (quick) ratio? Include Cash, Accounts Receivable, Short-term Investments, and Notes Receivable in your calculation. ____________

23. What is the total debt to stockholders' equity ratio (percentage)? ____________%

24. What is the return on beginning stockholder's equity for the quarter? No additional stock was sold during the quarter. (Use Net Income) ____________%

25. What is the carrying value of Notes Payable? $____________

26. What is the carrying value of the Long-term Lease Liability? $____________

27. If Ramblewood Manufacturing, Inc. has 100,000 shares of stock outstanding, what is the earnings per share (on Net Income) for the quarter? $____________

28. What is the equity per share on June 30, 1997? $____________

29. After closing, what is the balance of the Dividends Declared account? $____________

30. What was the net increase in Retained Earnings this quarter? $____________

31. Is the lease payment on June 30 for a capital lease or an operating lease? ____________

32. How much investment is "tied up" in the leasehold and leasehold improvements? $____________

33. Are any Ramblewood customers past due on their accounts? Remember that Ramblewood extends 30-day credit to all customers. YES______ NO______

34. Assuming a 30-day credit period is extended on receivables, how much cash should be collected the first 15 days of July? $____________

35. How much cash will be needed for accounts payable obligations the first 10 days of July? $____________

36. How much was paid (in total) to Ambrosini Steel, Inc. on June 24 and 26? $____________

37. If the June 24 and 26 payments to Ambrosini had not been paid on time to take the discount, what would have been the cost for this error? $____________
Remember that this invoice was recorded "NET".

FINAL EVALUATION
RAMBLEWOOD MANUFACTURING, INC.

38. Several invoices are due to be paid to River City Steel, Inc. The next two are due to be paid on what July dates? **July____and____**

Use the Schedule of Raw and In-Process Job Cards and the Individual Job Cards to answer the following questions.

39. How many jobs are currently in process? __________

40. How many jobs were completed and sold this month? __________

41. In April and May welding labor was charged at $50 per hour. Welding labor charges were increased by what percent on the June time tickets? __________**%**

42. In April and May four hours of welding labor charges resulted in what amount of total charges for overhead? **$**__________

43. To cover costs and improve profit margins, cutting and finishing hourly charges were increased sharply from $30 to $44 dollars per hour on the first of June. What was the percentage increase for this labor? __________**%**

Examine Job Card JOB22 to answer questions 44-47.

44. How many hours of cutting and finishing time were charged to JOB22? __________

45. Were all of the materials purchased from the same vendor? **YES**______**NO**______

46. What was the sales receipt number for this job? **Receipt Number**__________

47. If direct labor costs for JOB22 were increased by 10%, what would be the new total charge for manufacturing overhead? **$**__________

Examine Job Card JOB23 to answer questions 48-51

48. All but one of the material purchases for this job were acquired from the same vendor (Ambrosini Steel, Inc.). Identify the single purchase vendor. **Vendor**______________

49. How many hours of welding time were charged to the job? __________

50. Direct labor is what percent of the total cost of this job? __________**%**

51. Materials costing $19,120 were purchased for this job on June 16. If all of the tubing purchased on this order had been "up sized" to 1 1/2" tubing, what would have been the new total cost to complete JOB23? **$**__________

FINAL EVALUATION
RAMBLEWOOD MANUFACTURING, INC.

Examine Job Card JOB24 to answer questions 52-54.

52. How many total hours were charged to this job? ____________

53. On June 25 JOB24 sold for $1,975. What was the gross margin for this job? ____________%

54. If it was discovered after the sale that a time ticket totaling 10 hours of welding time and 4 hours of finishing time had not been recorded, what would have been the corrected total cost for the job? $____________

Examine Job Card JOB25 to answer questions 55-57.

55. What is the total charge for labor and overhead to-date? $____________

56. If this job was intended to sell at 45% above its cost, based on total costs to-date, what would be the retail selling price? $____________

57. If the materials could be purchased 7% lower from another vendor and 5% saved in total labor costs, how much would this lower the current cost of JOB25? $____________

Examine the Manufacturing Overhead ledger card.

58. What was the total amount of indirect materials charged to the Manufacturing Overhead account? $____________

59. What application rate applied on direct labor would have resulted in an underapplied balance of $68.71 in the Manufacturing Overhead account for the month of June? Remember that the $100.00 June 3 balance was from the months of April and May. ____________%

60. What percentage of manufacturing overhead charges for the month of June are attributed to indirect labor? ____________%

APPENDIX

Ramblewood Manufacturing, Incorporated
Trial Balance
June 2, 1997

	Accounts	Debit	Credit
101	Cash	$ 16,700.75	
103	Short-Term Investments	30,550.00	
105	Accounts Receivable	73,451.10	
109	Notes Receivable	32,000.00	
115	Raw and In-Process Inventory	6,975.00	
123	Prepaid Insurance	3,945.00	
124	Prepaid Rent	19,500.00	
129	Office Supplies	1,752.50	
131	Office Equipment	32,850.00	
132	Accum. Deprec., Office Equipment		$ 16,520.00
135	Shop Equipment	120,400.00	
136	Accum. Deprec., Shop Equipment		26,500.00
139	Trucks	45,600.00	
140	Accum. Deprec., Trucks		4,520.00
145	Leasehold Improvements	48,000.00	
160	Leasehold	45,000.00	
185	Manufacturing Overhead	100.00	
201	Accounts Payable		57,870.00
203	Notes Payable		36,000.00
207	Dividends Payable		15,000.00
231	Long-Term Lease Liability		6,500.00
232	Discount on Lease Financing	1,008.41	
301	Common Stock		250,000.00
305	Retained Earnings		47,602.81
311	Dividends Declared	15,000.00	
401	Custom Fencing and Gate Sales		217,512.00
501	Cost of Goods Sold	153,489.00	
602	Office Salaries and Wages Expense	10,012.00	
603	Truck Operating Expense	656.50	
604	Advertising Expense	1,575.00	
607	Credit Card Expense	40.00	
621	Rent Expense	1,200.00	
623	Bad Debt Expense	6,250.00	
625	Electric and Gas Expense	143.00	
626	Telephone Expense	112.00	
627	Bank Service Charges	40.00	
628	License Expense	251.00	
629	Professional Services Expense	502.00	
631	Miscellaneous Expense	95.00	
711	Interest Earned		426.00
713	Dividends Earned		97.00
721	Gain on Sale of Assets		127.00
731	Gain on Short-Term Investments		801.00
741	Miscellaneous Revenue		521.00
811	Income Tax Expense	11,800.00	
813	Interest Expense	576.40	
814	Discounts Lost	237.15	
821	Loss on Sale/Disposal of Assets	150.00	
831	Loss on Short-Term Investments	35.00	
Totals		$ 679,996.81	$ 679,996.81

Ramblewood Manufacturing, Incorporated
Schedule of Accounts Receivable
June 2, 1997

Customer Number	Customer Name	Account Balance
10400	Adams Construction Co.	$ 0.00
10650	Berline, Incorporated	0.00
10930	Fontaine Storage	1,250.65
11000	Lakeside Pools, Inc.	0.00
11150	Ralph E. Maxwell	14,000.00
11460	Sierra College	21,450.00
11680	Sutter County	36,750.45
11910	Wasaki Pool and Spa	0.00
Totals		$ 73,451.10

Ramblewood Manufacturing, Incorporated
Schedule of Accounts Payable
June 2, 1997

Vendor Number	Vendor Name	Account Balance
20500	Ambrosini Steel, Inc.	$ 0.00
21880	Delta Supply	0.00
22500	Golden Welding Supply	16,256.00
23400	Granite Business Supply	0.00
24800	Klondyke Air & Gas	0.00
25850	Loomis Legal Group	430.00
26575	River City Steel, Inc.	26,974.00
28500	Yamasaki Steel, Inc.	14,210.00
Totals		$ 57,870.00

Ramblewood Manufacturing, Incorporated
Schedule of Raw and In-Process Inventory Job Cards

Job Card	Total Cost To Date
JOB 19 Is Completed	
JOB 20 Ornamental Fencing	$ 6,975.00
Totals	$ 6,975.00